THE BEST 50
CHERRY RECIPES

Barbara Morgenroth

BRISTOL PUBLISHING ENTERPRISES
San Leandro, California

Printed in the United States of America.

ISBN 1-55867-197-8

Cover design: Frank J. Paredes
Cover photography: John A. Benson
Food styling: Susan Massey

ABOUT CHERRIES

Cherries have been cultivated since the time of the Assyrians and Babylonians. The word *cherry* derives from the classical Greek word *kerasos*. The family, or genus in botanical terms, is *prunus*, a lovely family to hail from. Other family members are plums, peaches, apricots, almonds and roses.

The hardier varieties of cherries were common in Britain and were cultivated as far north as Scandinavia. By the first century A.D., there were 10 varieties in Italy. The appreciation for cherries has never abated. By the time America was being colonized, 24 varieties were grown in England. Many types traveled with the settlers to the eastern seaboard and along the Saint Lawrence River. By 1847, cherries had made the trek west, arriving in Oregon with members of the Hudson Bay Company. Nearly 1,000 varieties of cherries are now cultivated worldwide.

- The *Bing cherry* is perhaps the variety most people are familiar with. Developed in 1875 by a grower in Milwaukie, Oregon, the Bing was named for one of his Chinese field workers.
- The *Queen Anne cherry,* a popular sweet variety, is nearly yellow with a pale blush of pink.
- The darkest cherry is the *Black Tartarian.*
- The cherry jam we love on our English muffins is commonly derived from the extremely sour *Morello cherry,* which is also used in the manufacturing of *kirschwasser* (cherry brandy).
- *Maraschino cherries,* the ones we find on top of our ice cream sundaes, are usually made from sour cherries. These cherries go through a 6-week processing period before being bottled.
- *Maraschino liqueur* is made from a wild Italian cherry called *marasca.*

Sometimes cherries are sold as *sour* or *sweet.* Sour cherries are said to hold their color and better flavor than sweet cherries during the cooking process, but in most recipes, sweet and sour cherries are interchangeable.

Cherries don't contain enough fat to talk about, so they are perfect for those watching their waistlines. One cherry contains about 5 calories. While they are a good source of fiber, cherries also provide vitamin C, calcium, magnesium, phosphorus and potassium.

Fresh cherries can be obtained in the late spring through summer in farmstands or supermarkets throughout the country. In general, the darker the color of the cherries, the sweeter the flavor will be. The storage life of fresh cherries is very short and they should be washed only just prior to using. Luckily, cherries freeze well, so we're able to enjoy this delicacy year round.

Most supermarkets carry canned white or red cherries. Sour cherries are usually found packed in jars and imported from Europe.

Frozen cherries can be found in supermarkets, but can also be obtained in 5-pound boxes through farm supply stores, such as Agway in the Northeast. Check with your feed store for a frozen food sale. Try a restaurant supply outlet for these large quantities, too.

Look for dried cherries in the specialty produce section of your supermarket. Warehouse stores like Costco sometimes carry dried fruits and berries. Or, try a gourmet store. Williams-Sonoma carries a range of dried fruits. Trader Joe's, a gourmet-sort of supermarket, carries dried Bing cherries. You can find these stores on the west coast and in several eastern states — it's definitely worth the trip.

A cherry pitter is a gadget with a small plunger that extracts the pit while keeping the fruit whole. It simplifies life considerably, but a paring knife will do the job, too.

CREAMED CHERRIES

Wondering how to make plain toast taste delectable? This is a terrific answer.

1 cup pitted cherries
¼ cup heavy cream
2 slices hearty white bread
dash cinnamon sugar

In a saucepan, heat cherries and cream over low heat until cream is slightly reduced. Toast bread until golden. Cut toast into triangles and arrange on a plate. Spoon cherry mixture over toast and sprinkle with cinnamon sugar.

Servings: 1

CHERRY PECAN BREAD

This delicious quick bread is easy and delicious.

1 cup milk
1 cup honey
½ cup butter
2½ cups all-purpose flour
½ tsp. salt
1 tbs. baking powder
2 eggs, beaten
½ cup dried cherries
½ cup chopped pecans

Heat oven to 325°. In a saucepan, heat milk, honey and butter until butter melts. In a large bowl, mix flour, salt and baking powder. Mix milk mixture and eggs with flour mixture until moistened. Fold in cherries and pecans and pour into a greased loaf pan. Bake for about 1 hour, until a knife inserted into the center of bread comes out clean. Cool in pan for 15 minutes.

Makes 1 loaf

CHERRY MUFFINS

This recipe makes use of dried cherries, giving the muffins a satisfying, chewy quality.

2 cups all-purpose flour
2 tsp. baking powder
½ tsp. salt
1 egg
¼ cup butter, melted
1½ cups milk, room temperature
¼ cup honey
½ cup dried cherries

Heat oven to 450°. In a bowl, mix flour, baking powder and salt. In another bowl, beat egg with butter, milk and honey. Add liquid ingredients to dry ingredients and add cherries. Stir just enough to moisten flour; do not overmix. Fill greased muffin cups ⅔ full and bake for 20 to 25 minutes, until golden brown.

Makes 12

ZINGY BINGY SOUP

A light summer lunch of crusty bread and creamy cheese is the perfect accompaniment for this soup. Or, serve this soup as a light dessert to end a long, hot day.

1 lb. fresh Bing cherries, pitted
½ cup black cherry juice
1 tsp. grated fresh orange
  peel (zest)
½ cup heavy cream
½ cup plain yogurt
¼ tsp. ground ginger
1 lime, sliced paper-thin
fresh mint leaves for garnish

Combine cherries, cherry juice, orange peel, cream, yogurt and ginger in a food processor workbowl and process until smooth. Transfer to a storage container and refrigerate for at least 8 hours to blend flavors. Garnish servings with a lime slice and mint leaf.

Servings: 4-6

CHERRY CARROT SALAD

This is a different take on an old favorite. The addition of seeds and nuts boosts both nutrition and taste. Look for flax seeds in a health food store. This can be made a day ahead if needed.

- 1/2 cup dried cherries
- 2 cups grated carrots
- 1/2 cup mayonnaise
- 2 tbs. lemon juice, or to taste
- 2 tbs. honey, or to taste
- 1/4 cup chopped walnuts
- 1/4 cup diced apple
- 1 tbs. sunflower kernels
- 2 tsp. flax seeds
- 1 tsp. dried parsley flakes

In a bowl, mix all ingredients together. Cover bowl with plastic wrap and refrigerate for at least 1 hour.

Servings: 4

YANKEE DOODLE STUFFED SQUASH

Autumn comes early in the Northeast, and with it comes a profusion of squash varieties. A particularly nice type is the black-skinned acorn, which lends itself well to a single serving. This side dish makes a delicious accompaniment to turkey or roast beef. You may need to adjust the baking time, depending on the size and age of the squash.

2 acorn squash
1 cup firm cooked rice
½ cup dried cherries
¼ cup unsalted butter, melted
1 Cortland or Granny Smith apple, peeled, cored and diced
1 tbs. light brown sugar
½ tsp. cinnamon
¼ cup water
salt and pepper to taste

Heat oven to 375°. Cut squash in half and scoop out seeds. Place squash halves in a baking dish cut-side down. Add about 1 inch water to pan and bake for about 1 hour. Turn squash over and bake until tender, about 45 minutes. Remove squash from oven and reduce oven heat to 325°. Scoop out squash flesh without tearing the shells and transfer to a large bowl. Mash squash flesh with a fork or potato masher and add rice and remaining ingredients. Mix ingredients together and spoon mixture into squash shells. Bake for about 20 minutes, until heated through.

Servings: 4

CHERRY PILAF

This makes an interesting side dish for a simple entrée.

1 small onion, chopped
olive oil
1 clove garlic, finely chopped
1 cup brown rice
1 cup chicken stock
1½ cups water
½ cup dried cherries
1 tbs. chopped fresh parsley
2 tbs. butter
salt and pepper to taste

In a large saucepan, sauté onion in a small amount of oil until tender. Add garlic and sauté briefly. Add rice, stock, water and dried cherries and bring to a boil. Cover pan, reduce heat to low and simmer mixture for about 45 minutes, until rice is tender. Remove pan from heat and stir in parsley and butter. Season with salt and pepper. Serve hot.

Makes 3 cups

CHERRY-GLAZED CHICKEN

We're all looking for new recipes for the same old bird. Roasting a chicken is easy food preparation: just put it in the oven and walk away; the bird does the rest.

1 roasting chicken, about 6 lb.
½ cup honey
½ cup cherry juice
1 tbs. lemon juice

Heat oven to 350°. Rinse chicken, pat dry and place in a roasting pan. Roast for 1 hour. Combine honey, cherry juice and lemon juice in a bowl and brush over chicken. Return chicken to oven, basting every 15 minutes until juices run clear when a thigh is pierced, about 60 minutes. Remove chicken from oven, let stand for about 10 minutes and carve into serving pieces.

Servings: 4-6

CHERRY-ROASTED PORK

Pork roast makes a good winter dinner. Using a plastic roasting bag makes a tender, juicy roast and creates a no-work gravy at the same time.

1 pork roast, about 4 lb.
salt and pepper to taste
1 cup dried cherries
1 cup dried apricots
1 cup dried apples
1 cup white wine
½ cup brown sugar, packed

Heat oven to 350°. Season pork with salt and pepper and slide into a plastic roasting bag; place bag in a roasting pan. Add dried fruit, wine and sugar to bag and seal bag according to package directions. Poke several holes in bag with the tip of a knife. Roast for about 20 minutes per pound, until a thermometer registers 160° when inserted into the thickest part of meat. Carefully remove pork from bag and place on a serving platter. Pour pan juices with fruit into a saucepan and heat over low heat until slightly reduced and thickened. Pour juices into a gravy boat to pass with sliced pork.

Servings: 6-8

KANSAS HAM AND CHERRY SAUCE

This is a wonderful meal for an autumn evening. It's a great way to use leftover ham.

- 1 baked ham, about 2 lb., thinly sliced
- 1 can (16 oz.) sweet cherries, drained, juice reserved
- 5 tsp. cornstarch
- 2 tsp. lemon juice
- ½ cup light brown sugar, packed
- ¼ tsp. diced candied ginger
- ⅛ tsp. cinnamon
- ⅛ tsp. nutmeg

Heat oven to 350°. Arrange ham slices in a baking dish. In a saucepan, combine cherry juice, cornstarch, lemon juice, sugar and spices. Cook over medium heat, stirring constantly, until liquid is thickened. Stir in cherries. Spoon cherry sauce over ham and bake for about 30 minutes, or until sauce is desired consistency.

Servings: 6

SOPHIE'S KIRSCH SCHNITZEL

Years ago, Sophie came to America on the Bremerhaven with little more than a dream and a treasure trove of family recipes. This is one of them. Kirsch is the German word for cherry.

- 4 veal cutlets, about 6 oz. each
- 1 tbs. canola oil
- ½ tsp. salt
- ⅛ tsp. white pepper
- ¼ cup dry red wine
- 2 tbs. heavy cream
- 1 can (16 oz.) sour cherries, drained

Pat cutlets dry. Heat oil in a skillet over medium-high heat. Brown cutlets on each side, about 3 minutes per side, and season with salt and pepper; transfer to a plate and keep warm. Add wine and cream to skillet, reduce heat to low and simmer for 3 minutes. Add cherries and heat through. Return veal to pan and coat with sauce; do not boil. Transfer veal to a platter and pour sauce over the top.

Servings: 4

CHERRY SALSA

Mexican food has captivated the nation's collective palate. Fruit salsas are new twists on the old favorite Mexican condiment; this one is a terrific blend of the old and the new.

- 1 cup pitted fresh cherries
- 1 tsp. grated fresh lime peel (zest)
- 2 tbs. lime juice
- 1/4 cup orange juice
- 2 tbs. olive oil
- 1/2 cup diced red onion
- 1 jalapeño pepper, seeded and minced
- 1 clove garlic, minced
- 1 red bell pepper, diced
- 1/4 cup chopped fresh cilantro

Combine all ingredients in a large bowl and blend well. Cover and chill for several hours to blend flavors. Remove from refrigerator and bring to room temperature before serving.

Makes about 2 cups

CHERRY DIP

This makes a tasty change from the usual dips. Serve with fresh fruit wedges for a lovely summer refresher.

½ cup pitted fresh or frozen cherries
(do not thaw frozen cherries)
6 oz. cream cheese, room temperature
1 tbs. sugar
¼ tsp. ground ginger
1½ tbs. lemon juice

Crush cherries, allowing some large pieces to remain. With an electric mixer, blend cream cheese, sugar and ginger in a bowl. Add lemon juice and blend well. Add cherries and mix until incorporated. Cover and refrigerate until ready to serve.

Makes about 1½ cups

CHERRY COULIS

A coulis is a sauce based on a fruit or vegetable puree. It has many uses, limited only to your imagination; this one's good over ice cream or cake. You can also use this in combination with other fruit sauces, such as kiwi or mango.

4 cups pitted fresh cherries
1 cup sugar
1½ cups orange juice
2 tbs. grated fresh orange peel (zest)
2 tbs. maraschino liqueur

Combine cherries, sugar, orange juice and orange peel in a large saucepan. Bring to a boil, reduce heat to low and simmer until cherries soften and mixture thickens slightly, about 8 to 10 minutes. Transfer mixture to a food processor workbowl and process until smooth. Stir in liqueur and mix well. Chill until ready to serve.

Makes about 2 cups

CHERRY RUM SAUCE

This is a wonderful topping for ice cream, but it is equally good over creamy custard or yogurt. The alcohol from the rum cooks off, leaving only its flavor behind.

- 2 cups pitted fresh sweet cherries
- ½ cup sugar
- 1 tbs. lemon juice
- 2 tbs. light rum
- 2 tsp. cornstarch
- 1 tbs. cold water

Simmer cherries, sugar and lemon juice in the top of a double boiler, until cherries are very soft. Add rum and mix well. Combine cornstarch and water and mix until smooth. Add cornstarch mixture to cherry mixture and stir until mixture thickens; cool. Chill for at least several hours before serving to blend flavors.

Makes about 2 cups

CHERRY VINEGAR

Flavored vinegars have become very popular. They can be used in a variety of ways and are especially good to add flavor to salad dressings. Try this in a marinade for chicken or pork.

1 cup pitted fresh cherries
2 cups white wine vinegar
¼ cup light honey

Place cherries in a large saucepan with vinegar. Bring mixture to a boil, stir in honey and strain. Discard cherries. Cool mixture. Transfer flavored vinegar to a sterilized bottle and seal well. Store in a cool, dark place. Let stand in a cool, dark place for 7 to 10 days before using.

Makes about 2½ cups

CHERRY CHUTNEY

This condiment is a nice replacement for cranberry sauce, especially if the main course is duck.

1 lb. fresh cherries, pitted
1 small red onion, finely chopped
¾ cup red wine vinegar
½ cup sugar
½ cup raisins
½ tsp. red pepper flakes, optional
¼ tsp. salt
⅓ cup coarsely chopped walnuts

Combine cherries, onion, vinegar, sugar, raisins, pepper flakes, if using, and salt in a medium saucepan. Bring mixture to a boil, reduce heat to low and simmer until thickened, about 25 minutes, stirring occasionally. Stir in walnuts and transfer to a bowl; cool. Cover and chill until ready to serve.

Makes about 2 cups

CHERRY JELLY

In this recipe, the addition of apples, which naturally contain pectin, enables the cherry juices to set up nicely without adding commercial pectin. This recipe can be multiplied almost indefinitely, hampered only by how huge your pot is. You will need at least ½ cup each of the cherry and apple juice; and for each ½ cup of the mixed juices you'll need ⅔ cup sugar. You'll also need a jelly bag, which can be found at a specialty food store. Or, you can substitute a colander lined with several layers of cheesecloth.

apples, washed, cored and crushed
fresh cherries, washed, pitted and crushed
sugar

Prick apples with a fork and place in a heavy nonaluminum saucepan. Cover pan and cook over low heat until apples are tender and juices run freely, about 15 minutes. Cook cherries in the same manner, but for only about 3 minutes. Pour apple and cherry juices separately into jelly bags and suspend bags over bowls until juices no longer drip through.

Measure juices, pour into a heavy nonaluminum saucepan and add the appropriate amount of sugar. Heat mixture until it registers 222° on a candy thermometer, skimming if necessary.

Cool juices slightly and pour into plastic freezer containers. Let stand uncovered until completely cooled. Cover and freeze until ready to use.

Yield: varies

RED AND WHITE JAM

Every so often you'll find a variety of luscious white cherries, such as Rainier, in the market. Grab them to make this wonderful jam.

2 cups pitted fresh sweet white cherries
2 cups raspberries
1 cup orange juice
3 cups sugar
1 tbs. grated fresh lemon peel (zest)
1 tbs. grated fresh orange peel (zest)

Crush or dice about ½ of the cherries and ½ of the raspberries and place all fruit in a large nonaluminum saucepan. Add orange juice, sugar and peels to pan and simmer over low heat for about 10 minutes, stirring frequently. Continue to cook until mixture is thick, about 20 minutes. Cool mixture slightly and pour into plastic freezer containers. Let stand uncovered until completely cooled. Cover and freeze until ready to use.

Makes about 6 cups

CHERRY PRESERVES

When there's a bountiful crop of cherries, we want to use all the fruit that we can. Preserving fruit is a traditional way of making the summer goodness last through the winter.

4 cups pitted fresh cherries
3 cups sugar

Place fruit in a large nonaluminum saucepan and add sugar. Stir to cover fruit with sugar. Heat mixture slowly, stirring frequently, until boiling. Boil for about 5 minutes. Test consistency of preserves by placing a spoonful on a plate. If mixture holds its shape, it's done. Cook for a few minutes longer if necessary. Cool mixture slightly and pour into plastic freezer containers. Let stand uncovered until completely cooled. Cover and freeze until ready to use.

Makes about 6 cups

CHERRY BUTTER

This delicious fruit butter can be prepared quickly and served the same morning for a wonderful brunch treat.

4 cups pitted fresh cherries
½ cup water
½ cup crushed pineapple
½ tsp. grated fresh lemon peel (zest)
1 tbs. lemon juice
½ tsp. grated fresh orange peel (zest)
1 tbs. orange juice
1 cup sugar

Place fruit in a nonaluminum saucepan and add remaining ingredients. Cook slowly until mixture is thick, about 15 to 20 minutes. Cool and refrigerate, or freeze for later use.

Makes about 6 cups

CHERRY MAPLE SYRUP

This is a delicious way to top French toast or pancakes. Try it over ice cream for a real treat.

- 1½ cups pure maple syrup
- 1 cup sugar
- ½ cup molasses
- 1 tsp. grated fresh orange peel (zest)
- juice of 2 oranges
- 1 tsp. grated fresh lemon peel (zest)
- juice of 2 lemons
- 1 cup pitted fresh sweet cherries
- 2 tbs. butter

Combine syrup, sugar, molasses, orange peel, orange juice, lemon peel and lemon juice in a saucepan. Bring mixture to a boil, reduce heat to low and simmer for 10 minutes, stirring constantly. Add cherries and cook until softened, about 3 minutes. Stir in butter.

Makes 2 cups

CHERRY OATMEAL COOKIES

This is a sturdy cookie, one which begs to be taken on a long hike, to a remote picnic or to a backyard treehouse.

1 cup butter, softened
½ cup dark brown sugar, packed
1 cup granulated sugar
1 egg
1 tsp. vanilla extract
1½ cups all-purpose flour
1 tsp. baking powder
1½ cups old-fashioned rolled oats
1 cup dried cherries

Heat oven to 350°. With a mixer, beat butter and sugars until light and creamy. Add egg and beat until incorporated. Add vanilla and mix well. In another bowl, mix flour with baking powder and transfer to bowl with butter-egg mixture; mix well. Add oats and mix well. Add cherries and mix until incorporated. Drop dough by spoonfuls onto a greased baking sheet 1½ to 2 inches apart. Bake for 10 minutes, or until lightly brown. Transfer to a wire rack to cool.

Makes about 5 dozen

CHERRY BISCOTTI

These twice-baked Italian cookies are good for dunking into coffee or enjoying with ice cream.

½ cup butter, softened
¾ cup sugar
2 eggs
1 tsp. vanilla extract
1 tsp. grated fresh lemon peel (zest)
2 cups all-purpose flour
1½ tsp. baking powder
¼ tsp. salt
⅔ cup dried cherries, soaked in a small amount of water for several hours
⅔ cup pine nuts

Heat oven to 350°. With a mixer, blend butter and sugar until light and creamy. Add eggs, vanilla and lemon peel and mix well. In a bowl, mix flour, baking powder and salt and gradually blend into butter mixture; mix well. Drain cherries and add to batter with pine nuts; mix well. Divide dough in half. Shape dough into two 2½-x-12-inch logs on a greased baking sheet, spaced 2 inches apart. Bake logs for about 30 minutes, until golden brown; cool slightly. With a serrated knife, cut each log into 1-inch slices. Lay slices flat on baking sheet. Return sheet to oven and bake for about 8 minutes, until golden. Turn cookies and bake for about 8 more minutes, until golden. Cool on a wire rack.

Makes about 3 dozen

CHEWY CHERRY BROWNIES

These brownies have everything good going for them: they're dark, chewy and fruity. Serve with a tall glass of icy cold milk.

½ cup butter, softened
1 cup sugar
2 eggs
½ cup all-purpose flour
6 tbs. unsweetened cocoa powder
½ tsp. salt
1 tsp. vanilla extract
½ cup dried cherries
2 oz. bittersweet chocolate, chopped

Heat oven to 350°. With a mixer, blend butter and sugar until light and creamy. Add eggs and blend well. Add flour, cocoa, salt and vanilla extract and mix until blended. Add cherries and chopped chocolate and mix well. Pour mixture into a greased 8-x-8-inch baking pan. Bake for 30 minutes, or until just done; do not overbake. Cool and cut into squares.

NOTE: if using a glass baking dish, reduce oven heat to 325°.

Makes 9

CHERRY PIE

No wonder Mrs. Washington was so annoyed when George cut down the cherry tree. It might have been that very act that allowed apple pie to become the definitive American icon. Here's a pie that will give that old favorite a run for its money.

1 qt. fresh tart cherries, pitted
1¼ cups sugar
2½ tbs. all-purpose flour
¼ tsp. salt
Lemon Pastry, follows
1 tbs. butter

Heat oven to 450°. In a bowl, mix cherries with sugar, flour and salt. Line a 9-inch pie pan with ½ of the *Lemon Pastry*. Pour in cherry mixture, dot with butter and cover with remaining pastry. Crimp edges and make several steam vents in top crust with a small knife. Bake for 10 minutes. Set oven control to 350° and bake for 25 minutes. Cool on a rack.

LEMON PASTRY

2 cups all-purpose flour
1 tsp. salt
½ tsp. grated fresh lemon peel (zest)
⅔ cup vegetable shortening
1 tbs. lemon juice
4-6 tbs. ice-cold water

Combine flour and salt in a bowl, add lemon peel and mix well. With a pastry blender or 2 knives, cut in shortening until pieces are the size of small peas. Add lemon juice to flour mixture and mix gently. Add water, 1 tbs. at a time, until all flour mixture is moistened; do not overmix. Divide dough in half and wrap each half with waxed paper. Refrigerate for 30 minutes. On a lightly floured work surface, roll each dough piece into a ⅛-inch-thick round.

Makes one 9-inch double-crust pie

EASIEST CHERRY CAKE

When you want a quick and easy cake, this is the one to make. Tender and buttery, the cake is a lovely partner to large, juicy cherries.

½ cup butter, softened
1 cup sugar
2 eggs
1¾ cups all-purpose flour
¼ tsp. salt
1½ tsp. baking powder
½ cup milk
1 cup pitted fresh sweet cherries
sweetened whipped cream for garnish, optional

Heat oven to 350°. With a mixer, blend butter and sugar until light and creamy. Add eggs and beat well. In a bowl, mix together flour, salt and baking powder. Add ½ of the dry ingredients and ½ of the milk to butter mixture and mix well. Add remaining flour and milk and beat for about 2 minutes. Pour batter into a buttered and floured 8-inch square pan. Cover the top of batter with cherries. Bake for about 25 minutes, or until light golden brown and a toothpick inserted into the center of cake comes out clean. Cool. Serve plain or with a dollop of whipped cream.

Servings: 4-6

ENGLISH COUNTRY SWEET CAKE

This treat also goes by the name "Cut and Come Again." You will, too, once you try this British delectable.

½ cup whole milk
2 tbs. yeast
½ cup butter
1 cup all-purpose flour
¼ tsp. baking soda
½ tsp. nutmeg
½ tsp. ground ginger
½ cup light brown sugar, packed
½ cup dried cherries
¼ cup chopped candied cherries
¼ cup ground almonds
¼ tsp. almond extract

Heat oven to 300°. In a heavy saucepan, heat milk to 110°. Add yeast and let stand for several minutes. In a bowl, cut butter into flour with a pastry blender or 2 knives until mixture resembles cornmeal. Add baking soda, nutmeg, ginger, brown sugar, dried cherries, candied cherries, almonds and almond extract and mix well. Pour milk mixture into flour mixture and mix until well incorporated. Transfer mixture to a buttered and floured 8-inch square baking pan. Bake for about 35 minutes, or until a toothpick inserted into the center of cake comes out clean. Remove cake from oven and cool slightly before inverting onto a cooling rack. Cool before serving.

Servings: 4-6

CHERRY TIRAMISU

In Italian, tiramisu means "pick me up." While tiramisu is most often made with coffee, this recipe is a fruitful approach to a new classic. Mascarpone cheese is a very rich, almost sweet cream cheese that comes from Italy. Look for it in specialty supermarkets or gourmet stores. The number of layers will depend on the size and shape of the bowl or dish you are using.

8 oz. mascarpone cheese, room temperature
2 tbs. superfine sugar
½ tsp. vanilla extract
12 ladyfingers
3 tbs. kirschwasser (cherry brandy)
2 cups pitted fresh cherries, drained
1 cup heavy cream, whipped, for garnish
chopped pistachio nuts for garnish

In a bowl, blend mascarpone, sugar and vanilla until very smooth. In a glass bowl or baking dish, arrange a layer of ladyfingers. Drizzle or brush kirschwasser over ladyfingers. Spoon a layer of cherries on top and spread 1/3 to 1/2 of the mascarpone mixture over cherries. Repeat layering process until all ladyfingers have been used. Garnish with whipped cream and dust with chopped pistachios. Chill until ready to serve.

Servings: 4-6

CHERRY CLAFOUTI

This custard-like dessert is a traditional French offering. In France's Limousin region, the cherries used are often the first of the season and are left unpitted.

1/3 cup all-purpose flour
1/2 tsp. baking powder
6 oz. butter, melted
5 eggs, room temperature
1 cup milk
dash salt
1/4 cup sugar
1/4 cup kirschwasser (cherry brandy), optional
1/2 lb. fresh sweet black cherries, pitted or unpitted
2 tbs. sugar

Heat oven to 375°. Butter the bottom and sides of a shallow baking dish. Combine flour and baking powder in a bowl. Whisk in enough melted butter to create a smooth paste. Stir in remaining butter. Add eggs to bowl and beat well for 2 minutes. Add milk, salt, 1/4 cup sugar and 1/2 of the kirschwasser, if using. Mix well until batter is smooth and creamy. Gently mix cherries into batter, including cherry juice, if any. Transfer batter to baking dish and bake for 45 minutes, until puffed and golden. Sprinkle with remaining kirschwasser, if using, and 2 tbs. sugar. Serve warm or cold.

Servings: 4-6

CHERRY CRÈME BRULÉE

Crème brulée is among the ultimate of luxuries. The addition of cherries only heightens the taste sensation. Using the blond-colored, granular turbinado sugar helps to create a nice caramelized crust.

10 oz. fresh sweet cherries, halved
2 tbs. kirschwasser (cherry brandy)
5 large egg yolks
1/3 cup granulated sugar
1 1/2 cups heavy cream
1/4 cup milk
6 tsp. turbinado (raw) sugar

Place cherries in a saucepan and drizzle with kirschwasser. Cover and cook over low heat until cherries are tender, stirring often, about 8 minutes. Remove from heat and cool. Cover and refrigerate until ready to use.

Heat oven to 325°. Beat yolks with sugar in a large bowl and whisk in remaining ingredients. Divide mixture among six 2⁄3-cup baking dishes or ramekins and place dishes in a large baking pan. Pour water into pan to come 3⁄4 inch up the sides of dishes. Bake for 1 hour, or until eggs are just set. Remove baking dishes from pan and cool. Cover and chill for about 6 hours.

Heat broiler. Divide cherries among dishes and sprinkle each with 1 tsp. of the turbinado sugar. Broil until sugar melts and bubbles, about 1 minute. Cool slightly and serve.

Servings: 6

CHERRY CUSTARD COBBLER

This is a new twist on the old favorite. The custard sets up by itself and removes the need for any sauce.

1½ cups plus 1 tbs. all-purpose flour
1½ tsp. salt
½ cup butter
2½ cups pitted fresh dark sweet cherries
⅓ cup honey
½ tsp. cinnamon
1 egg
1 cup milk
¼ tsp. nutmeg
water, if needed

Heat oven to 375°. In a bowl, mix 1½ cups flour, salt and butter until coarse crumbs with a pastry blender or 2 knives. Press mixture into the bottom and halfway up the sides of an 8-inch square baking dish. Arrange cherries on crust, reserving juice if any. Mix honey with cinnamon and 1 tbs. flour and drizzle over cherries. Bake for 20 minutes and remove from oven. Beat egg in a bowl. Add milk, nutmeg and ½ cup reserved cherry juice. (If reserved cherry juice does not equal ½ cup, add water). Pour liquid over cherries. Return to oven and bake for 30 minutes.

Servings: 4

CHERRY-WALNUT CRISP

When you're in a rush, but still want something warm and delicious for dessert, don't look any further than this.

½ cup butter
½ cup all-purpose flour
½ cup sugar
3 cups pitted fresh cherries
dash cinnamon
½ cup chopped walnuts
¼ tsp. salt
unsweetened whipped cream

Heat oven to 350°. With a pastry blender or 2 knives, cut butter into flour and sugar until mixture resembles cornmeal. Place cherries, walnuts, salt and cinnamon in a buttered 2-quart baking dish and stir to combine. Spoon flour mixture over cherry mixture and bake for about 30 minutes, until topping is light golden brown and cherries are bubbling; cool slightly. Serve with whipped cream.

Servings: 4-6

CHERRY COTTAGE PUDDING

This dessert is more familiar to Grandmother than to us, and more's the pity. It's delicious served with lemon sauce.

1¾ cups all-purpose flour
½ tsp. salt
2½ tsp. baking powder
¼ cup butter, softened
1 cup sugar
1 egg
1 tsp. vanilla extract
⅔ cup milk
1 cup diced fresh cherries

Heat oven to 350°. Sift flour, salt and baking powder together. With a mixer, mix butter and sugar until light and creamy. Beat in egg and vanilla. Add milk to butter mixture alternately with flour mixture and beat until smooth. Add cherries and stir gently. Pour mixture into a greased 8-inch square baking dish. Bake for 30 to 45 minutes, until golden brown.

Servings: 4-6

CHERRY SOUFFLÉ

This recipe easily adapts to canned or frozen cherries. To make cherry pulp, process pitted cherries with a food processor until finely chopped.

1 cup cherry pulp
1 tbs. lemon juice
1⁄8 tsp. salt
sugar to taste
3 egg whites
custard sauce or whipped cream

Heat oven to 375°. Press cherries through a sieve into a bowl and add lemon juice, salt and sugar. Transfer mixture to a saucepan and heat through. Beat egg whites until stiff and fold into hot cherry mixture. Pour mixture into a greased baking dish or individual molds, filling 3⁄4 full. Set dish in a pan of hot water and bake for 20 minutes. If you prefer a firmer soufflé, bake at 325° for 40 minutes. Serve immediately with custard sauce or whipped cream.

Servings: 6

CHEERY CHERRY CHRISTMAS PUDDING

Puddings are a traditional dessert during the Christmas season, but the use of dried cherries is thoroughly modern.

- ½ cup dry sherry
- 1 tsp. lemon juice
- ½ cup dried cherries
- ½ cup chopped pecans
- 6 egg whites
- ½ cup sugar
- vanilla ice cream or custard sauce

Heat oven to 350°. In a bowl, mix sherry and lemon juice. Stir in cherries and pecans and let stand covered overnight.

The next day, beat egg whites until stiff and mix in sugar. Fold in cherry and nut mixture. Pour mixture into a buttered baking dish and set in a pan of hot water. Bake for 1 hour, until a toothpick inserted into the center comes out clean. Serve with ice cream or custard sauce.

Servings: 4-6

CHERRY BREAD PUDDING

Bread pudding is definitely comfort food.
It's delicious anytime, but especially when you
crave something warm and indulgent.

3 eggs
3 egg yolks
¾ cup sugar
dash salt
2 cups milk
1 cup heavy cream
1 inch vanilla bean
2 cups pitted fresh or frozen cherries
8-10 slices pound cake, crusts removed
½ tsp. freshly grated nutmeg
lightly sweetened whipped cream or vanilla ice cream, optional

Heat oven to 350°. In a bowl, whisk eggs, egg yolks, sugar and salt until well blended. Pour milk and cream into a large, heavy-bottomed saucepan with vanilla bean. Heat liquid until steaming and remove from heat. Slowly whisk hot milk mixture into egg yolk mixture; cool and strain. Place cherries in a lightly buttered baking dish. Arrange slices of pound cake on top of fruit and pour egg mixture over cake. Sprinkle with nutmeg. Bake pudding for about 1 hour, or until eggs are set; cool. If desired, serve with whipped cream or vanilla ice cream.

Servings: 8

HUNGARIAN FRIED CHERRIES

The Hungarian people take full advantage of the cherry season. A pyramid of fried cherries can be quite a spectacular sight if used as a centerpiece and decorated for the season. To make vanilla sugar, place a whole vanilla bean in a covered jar with 2 cups sugar. Let stand for at least 2 weeks before using.

½ cup all-purpose flour
2 eggs
1 tbs. confectioners' sugar
1 tbs. rum
dash salt, optional
about ½ cup canola oil for frying
1 lb. large fresh black cherries with stems
confectioners' sugar
vanilla sugar for dusting

In a bowl, combine flour, eggs, 1 tbs. confectioners' sugar, rum and salt, if using, and blend until just smooth. Let stand for 1 hour.

Heat oil in a skillet until hot. Reduce heat to low. Holding each by the stem, dip cherries into batter and place carefully in hot oil. Using the stems as handles, turn cherries carefully until crisp and light brown on all sides. Drain on paper towels. Roll warm fried cherries in confectioners' sugar and arrange in a pyramid on a plate. Dust with vanilla sugar.

Servings: 10

INDEPENDENCE DAY ICE CREAM

This ice cream is red, white and blue in honor of Independence Day. The use of dried blueberries prevents the colors from running together.

3 cups heavy cream
1 cup whole milk
¾ cup sugar
2 tbs. almond extract
4 egg yolks
¼ cup dried blueberries, soaked overnight in milk to cover
1 cup halved fresh black cherries

Heat cream, milk and sugar in a heavy saucepan over low heat until steaming and stir until sugar is dissolved. Whisk egg yolks in a bowl. Pour 1 cup of the hot milk mixture into bowl with yolks, whisking constantly. When smooth, slowly incorporate egg mixture into saucepan, stirring constantly. Cook over medium heat, whisking until mixture thickens slightly, about 8 minutes; do not let mixture boil. Cool mixture completely. Drain blueberries and add to ice cream mixture with cherries and almond extract. Freeze according to manufacturer's directions for your ice cream maker.

Makes about 1 quart

BING CHERRY SORBET

Just around mid-winter, residents of the upper tier of states start feeling deprived. The weather's cold, everything tasty and delightful seems to be unavailable and spring seems months away. What a treat this is on a snowy evening when cherries are out of season!

2 cans (16 oz. each) pitted Bing cherries in heavy syrup
2 cups *Simple Syrup*, page 62
1/4 cup lemon juice
1/4 cup water
lemons, optional

Drain cherries, reserving 2 tbs. of the cherry syrup. Press fruit through a food mill or process with a blender until smooth. Stir in reserved cherry syrup, simple syrup, lemon juice and water. Freeze according to manufacturer's directions for your ice cream maker.

If desired, cut lemons in half and slice off ends so that fruit stands on its own. Scoop out lemon pulp and reserve for another use. Freeze shells until firm. Fill shells with sorbet and store in the freezer until ready to serve.

Makes about 4½ cups

SIMPLE SYRUP

Simple syrup can be used to sweeten lemonade, iced tea or sorbet. Using it assures that you'll never have granules of undissolved sugar in your summer drinks or sorbets.

4 cups water
4 cups sugar

Combine water and sugar in a saucepan. Heat until sugar dissolves; cool. Store in a covered container in the refrigerator.

Makes about 1 quart

CHERRY PARFAIT

Ice cream is a delicacy that's hard to pass up, but this is an improvement on a wonderful treat. You can easily expand this recipe to accommodate any number of people.

1 scoop cherry ice cream, softened slightly
whipped cream to taste
pitted fresh dark cherries to taste
shaved dark chocolate to taste

Place ice cream and 1 large spoonful whipped cream in a bowl; blend thoroughly. Transfer mixture to a parfait glass. Add a layer of fresh cherries and top with a dollop of whipped cream. Garnish with shaved chocolate.

Servings: 1

CHERRY PRALINE YOGURT

This is a treat that even children love. The fat is kept to a minimum, but the taste is extraordinary. Use fresh or canned cherries.

1/3 cup sugar
1/3 cup pecans, or to taste
8 oz. nonfat plain yogurt
1/2 cup pitted sweet cherries
grated fresh orange peel (zest) to taste, optional
fresh mint for garnish

In a heavy skillet or saucepan, melt sugar over medium-high heat, stirring constantly until it begins to turn brown. Add pecans and quickly stir until nuts are completely coated. Transfer nuts to waxed paper and cool. In a bowl, combine yogurt, cherries and orange zest, if using. Stir briefly. Add candied pecans and stir briefly. Serve in a bowl garnished with mint.

Servings: 1

WINTER FRUIT COMPOTE

Not only is this a delightful dessert, the aroma will waft through the entire house as you make it. Serve it at any temperature, alone or over a buttery pound cake.

1 cup dried cherries
1 cup dried apples
1 cup dried apricots
½ cup dried prunes
½ cup dried blueberries
8 cups water
2 sticks cinnamon
½ cup almonds, chopped into large pieces
¼ tsp. grated fresh orange peel (zest)
few allspice berries
dash mace

Combine all ingredients in a saucepan and bring to a boil. Reduce heat to low, cover and simmer for 45 minutes. Remove allspice.

Servings: 4-6

CHERRY COMPOTE

Mascarpone is an Italian cream cheese with many uses. It is commonly used in the very popular dessert tiramisu. Mascarpone can also be used as a replacement for buttercream frosting or whipped cream, as with this compote.

¾ cup red Zinfandel wine, water or cherry juice
3 tbs. sugar
½ vanilla bean, split
1 lb. fresh cherries, pitted
2 tbs. dried cherries
1 pkg. (5 oz.) mascarpone cheese, room temperature
1½ tbs. milk
1 tbs. confectioners' sugar

In a large saucepan, combine wine, sugar and vanilla bean. Bring to a boil, reduce heat to low and simmer for 4 minutes. Add fresh cherries and dried cherries to pan and simmer for 5 minutes. Remove cherries with a slotted spoon and transfer to a bowl. Bring liquid to a boil and cook until thickened, about 5 minutes. Pour liquid over cherries in bowl; cool. Cover and refrigerate cherry mixture overnight. In a bowl, whisk mascarpone with milk and confectioners' sugar. Cover and refrigerate overnight.

Bring mascarpone mixture to room temperature. Remove vanilla bean from cherry mixture. Divide cherry mixture among dessert bowls and dollop with mascarpone mixture.

Servings: 6

CHERRY SYRUP

To serve, pour several spoonfuls of syrup into a large glass, fill with icy cold water or seltzer and garnish with a sprig of mint. Look for fresh currants at specialty markets.

3 lb. fresh sour cherries, pitted
1 lb. fresh red currants
1 lb. raspberries
sugar as needed

Crush fruits in a large container, cover and let stand in a warm place for about 24 hours. The following day, strain liquid, measure and pour into a large stainless steel or enamel pot. Add 4 cups sugar for every 2½ cups liquid to pot and bring to a boil. Reduce heat to low and simmer until sugar is completely dissolved, about 15 to 20 minutes. Cool and skim. Pour syrup into sterilized bottles or containers and seal well. Refrigerate for as long as 1 month; once opened, use within 2 weeks.

Makes about 7 cups

BRANDIED CHERRIES

You can find these imported delicacies in gourmet food shops, but it's easy and more economical to prepare them at home. Serve them over ice cream or use for baking.

3 lb. fresh cherries, pitted
cognac
¼ lb. sugar
3 tbs. water

Pack cherries firmly into sterilized wide-mouthed canning jars. Cover with cognac, seal well and store in a cool, dark place for 6 weeks.

Drain liquid from cherries. In a bowl, mix sugar with water and cherry liquid, stirring until sugar is dissolved. Strain liquid and pour over cherries in jars. Reseal jars and store until ready to use.

Makes about 3 pints

CANDIED CHERRIES

For those concerned with artificial flavorings and colorings, look no further than your own pantry shelf for candied cherries.

2 cups sugar
1 cup water
⅓ cup light corn syrup
3 cups pitted fresh cherries

In a large saucepan, place sugar, water and corn syrup. Bring mixture to a boil and cook until mixture reaches 234° on a candy thermometer. Add cherries to boiling syrup, taking care that fruit isn't crowded. Simmer until cherries are translucent. With a slotted spoon, remove cherries from syrup and drain. Spread cherries on a screen and air-dry until no longer sticky, about 3 days. Store cherries in a covered container between sheets of waxed paper. Use within 3 months.

Makes about 2 cups

CRYSTALLIZED CHERRIES

This simple treat is both quick and delicious.
Serve as a garnish, topping or dessert.

1 cup pure maple syrup
1 cup water
2 cups pitted fresh sweet cherries

Pour maple syrup and water into a large saucepan and bring to a boil. Cook for about 10 minutes. Add cherries and simmer for 15 minutes, until water evaporates and maple syrup begins to crystallize around fruit. Remove from heat and cool.

Makes about 1 cup

SEASON'S GREETINGS FUDGE

This is a festive fudge for the holidays. It tastes as good as it looks and will serve all the carolers who show up at your door. For a festive treat, use small cookie cutters and cut the fudge into holiday shapes.

1½ cup heavy cream
1 cup light corn syrup
¼ cup butter
3 cups sugar
1 tsp. vanilla extract
1 cup candied red cherries
1 cup candied green cherries
1 cup macadamia nuts
1 cup pecans
1 cup walnuts

In a large saucepan, combine cream, corn syrup, butter and sugar. Bring to a boil over medium heat, stirring frequently, and cook until mixture registers 238° on a candy thermometer. Remove mixture from heat and cool until the temperature of mixture drops to 200°. With a wooden spoon, beat mixture until it thickens and lightens in color, about 3 minutes. Stir in vanilla, cherries and nuts until incorporated. Transfer mixture to a buttered 9-x-13-inch pan and refrigerate until completely cool and firm. With a sharp knife, cut fudge into small squares.

Makes about 2 pounds

CHERRY CHOCOLATE CORDIALS

One of the most delightful and decadent treats in the world is a liqueur-filled chocolate. Use the finest dark chocolate you can find and the results will transport you to another dimension.

12 oz. best-quality dark chocolate, such as Callebaut or Valhrona
24 candied cherries
3 tbs. kirschwasser (cherry brandy)
1½ tbs. cherry syrup, such as Torani

Chop chocolate finely and melt in the top of a double boiler (be careful not to heat too much or consistency of chocolate will be affected). Maintain the temperature of chocolate near 110° throughout the candy-making process. Spoon enough melted chocolate into small foil candy cups or plastic cordial molds to cover the bottom. Chill for 5 minutes. Place 1 cherry in each chocolate cup and pour a small amount of kirschwasser and syrup over each cherry. Spoon enough chocolate over each cherry to cover and chill for 5 minutes. Remove chocolate-covered cherries from molds or foil cups and transfer to a baking sheet lined with aluminum foil or waxed paper. Spoon a second coating of chocolate over each cordial and chill until firm. Store in a cool, dry place.

Serves a few chocoholics or 2 dozen others

INDEX